FARM MACHINES

PLANTER

KATHY MIDDLETON

A Crabtree Roots Book

Crabtree Publishing
crabtreebooks.com

School-to-Home Support for Caregivers and Teachers

This book helps children grow by letting them practice reading. Here are a few guiding questions to help readers build comprehension skills. Possible answers appear here in red.

Before Reading:

- What do I think this book is about?
    - *I think this book is about planters.*
    - *I think this book will talk about what planters do.*
- What do I want to learn about this topic?
    - *I want to learn about what jobs planters do.*
    - *I want to learn why planters are important farm machines.*

During Reading:

- I wonder why...
    - *I wonder why farmers use planters.*
    - *I wonder why planters are needed on the farm.*
- What have I learned so far?
    - *I have learned that planters have hoppers that hold seeds.*
    - *I have learned that planters have many small wheels.*

After Reading:

- What details did I learn about this topic?
    - *I have learned that planters attach to a tractor.*
    - *I learned that planters plant seeds in straight rows.*
- Read the book again and look for the vocabulary words.
    - *I see the word* ***planter*** *on page 3 and the word* ***hopper*** *on page 8. The other vocabulary words are found on page 14.*

This is a **planter**.

A planter plants seeds in fields on a farm.

A planter attaches to a **tractor**.

All planters have **hoppers** that hold the seeds.

Many small **wheels** cover the seeds with soil.

Planters plant seeds in **straight** rows.

Word List

Sight Words

a
all
attaches
cover
farm
fields
have
holds
in
is
many
on
plants
rows
soil
small
that
the
this
to
with

Words to Know

hoppers

planter

straight

tractor

wheels

41 Words

This is a **planter**.

A planter plants seeds in fields on a farm.

A planter attaches to a **tractor**.

All planters have **hoppers** that hold the seeds.

Many small **wheels** cover the seeds with soil.

Planters plant seeds in **straight** rows.

FARM MACHINES PLANTER

Written by: Kathy Middleton
Designed by: Under the Oaks Media
Proofreader: Crystal Sikkens
Production manager: Candice Campbell
Prepress technician: Katherine Kantor

Photographs: All images from Sutterstock

Crabtree Publishing

crabtreebooks.com 800-387-7650

In Canada: We acknowledge the financial support of the Government of Canada through the Canada Book Fund for our publishing activities.

Printed in the U.S.A./CP2025

Published in Canada
Crabtree Publishing
616 Welland Ave.
St. Catharines, Ontario
L2M 5V6

Published in the United States
Crabtree Publishing
347 Fifth Ave
Suite 1402-145
New York, NY 10016

Library and Archives Canada Cataloguing in Publication
Available at Library and Archives Canada

Library of Congress Cataloging-in-Publication Data
Available at the Library of Congress

Hardcover: 978-1-0398-8101-3
Paperback: 978-1-0398-8462-5
Ebook (pdf): 978-1-0398-8221-8
Epub: 978-1-0398-8341-3
Audio: 978-1-0398-8504-2
Read-Along: 978-1-0398-8546-2